ANIMAL
CAMOUFLAGE

First edition for the United States, Canada,
and the Philippines published 1991
by Barron's Educational Series, Inc.

Design David West Children's Book Design
Illustrations Kate Taylor
Text Anita Ganeri
Picture research Angela Graham

Created and designed by
N.W. Books
28 Percy Street
London W1P 9FF

All inquiries should be addressed to:
Barron's Educational Series, Inc.
250 Wireless Boulevard
Hauppauge, NY 11788

International Standard Book No. 0-8120-6236-1

Library of Congress Catalog Card No. 91-9985

Library of Congress Cataloging-in Publication Data

Ganeri, Anita. 1961-
Camouflage / by Anita Ganeri : illustrated by Kate Taylor.
p.   cm. -- (Animal questions and answers)
Summary: Questions and answers reveal how different
animals use camouflage to protect themselves.
ISBN 0-8120-6236-1
1. Camouflage (Biology)--Miscellanea--Juvenile
literature. 2. Mimicry (Biology)--Miscellanea--Juvenile
literature. [1. Camouflage (Biology)--Miscellanea. 2.
Animal defenses--Miscellanea. 3. Questions and
answers.] I. Taylor, Kate, ill. II. Title. III. Series.
QL767.G36   1991
591.57'2--dc20   91-9985   CIP   AC

Printed in Belgium
1234   987654321

QUESTIONS AND ANSWERS ABOUT
ANIMAL
CAMOUFLAGE

Barron's

New York • Toronto

Why do animals use camouflage?

Camouflage is a disguise animals use to avoid being seen by their enemies or by their prey. Sometimes, the color of an animal's hair or feathers matches its background so it is difficult to see. Some animals can even change color to blend in with different backgrounds. Other animals hide by looking like something else. This book will tell you about many of the clever ways animals have of hiding themselves.

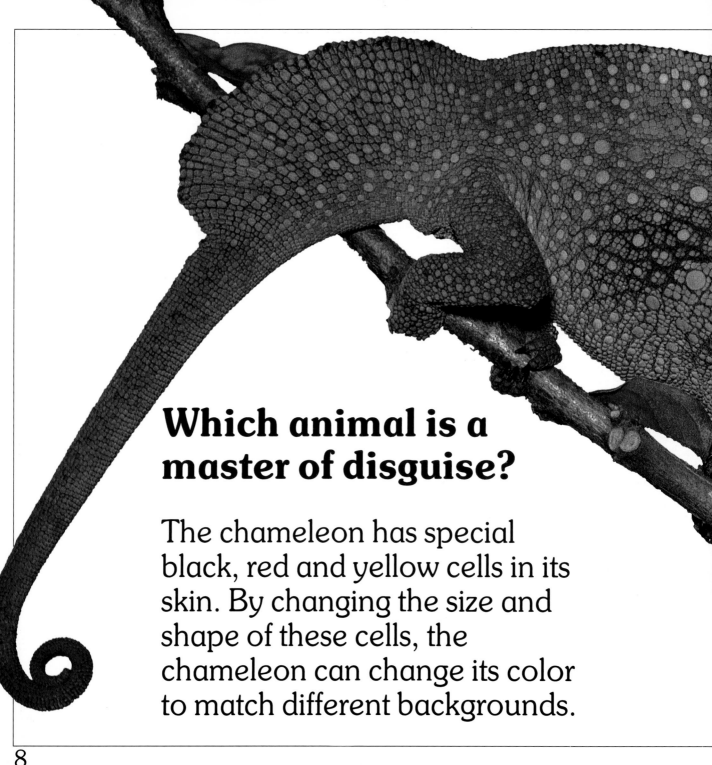

Which animal is a master of disguise?

The chameleon has special black, red and yellow cells in its skin. By changing the size and shape of these cells, the chameleon can change its color to match different backgrounds.

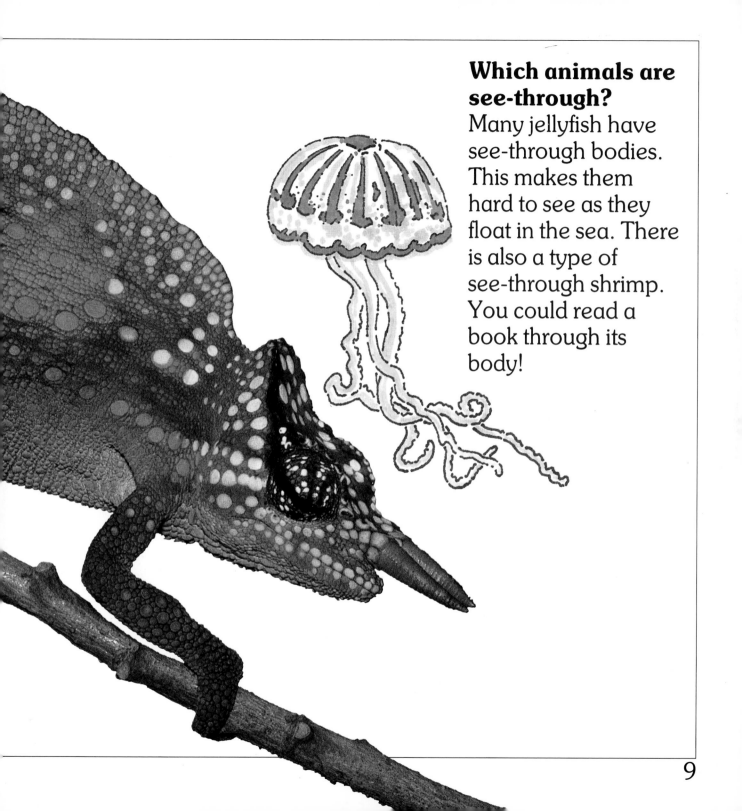

Which animals are see-through?

Many jellyfish have see-through bodies. This makes them hard to see as they float in the sea. There is also a type of see-through shrimp. You could read a book through its body!

9

Why are zebras striped?

No one really knows if a zebra's stripes are for camouflage. A lion can easily pick out a single zebra to kill. But when a group of zebras start running, their stripes make them much harder to see.

Why do some animals have spotted coats?

The patches on a giraffe's coat help hide it. They blend in with patches of light and shade, making the giraffe difficult to see among trees despite its strange shape!

Which twigs are really insects?

Stick insects make tasty meals for hungry birds. But the insects are not easy to spot. Their bodies are long, thin and green or brown. They look just like the twigs they hang on.

Which animals look like flowers?

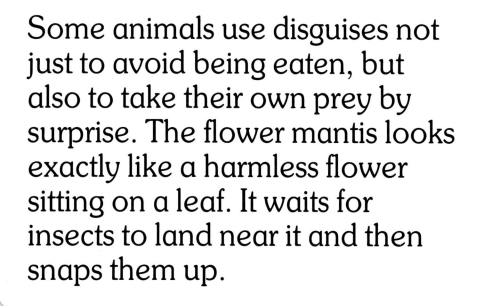

Some animals use disguises not just to avoid being eaten, but also to take their own prey by surprise. The flower mantis looks exactly like a harmless flower sitting on a leaf. It waits for insects to land near it and then snaps them up.

How do animals use colors as warnings?

In nature, red, yellow and black are used as warning colors. They tell other animals to keep well away. The colors of the arrow-poison frog warn predators that it is poisonous to eat. A single drop of its poison is enough to kill a monkey.

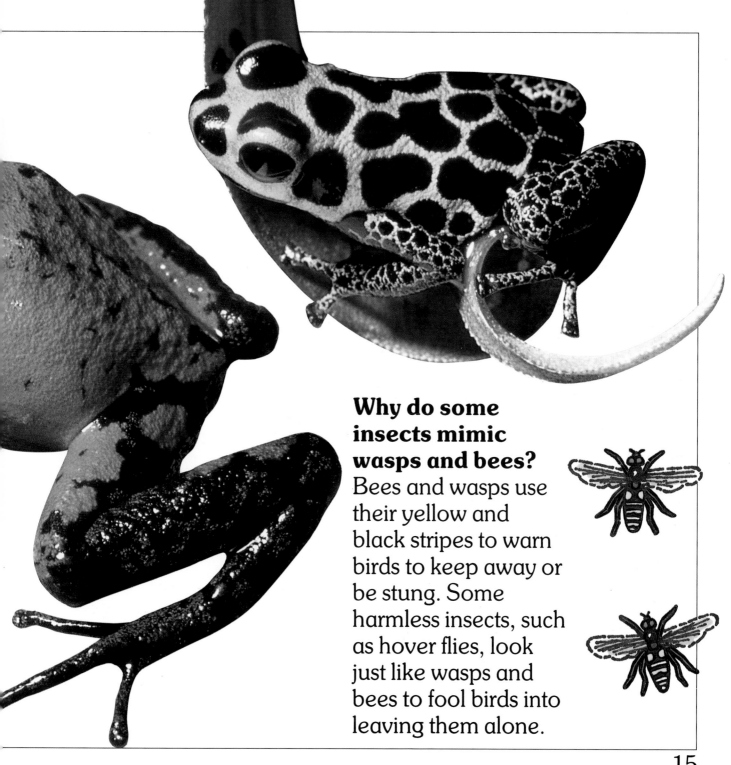

Why do some insects mimic wasps and bees?

Bees and wasps use their yellow and black stripes to warn birds to keep away or be stung. Some harmless insects, such as hover flies, look just like wasps and bees to fool birds into leaving them alone.

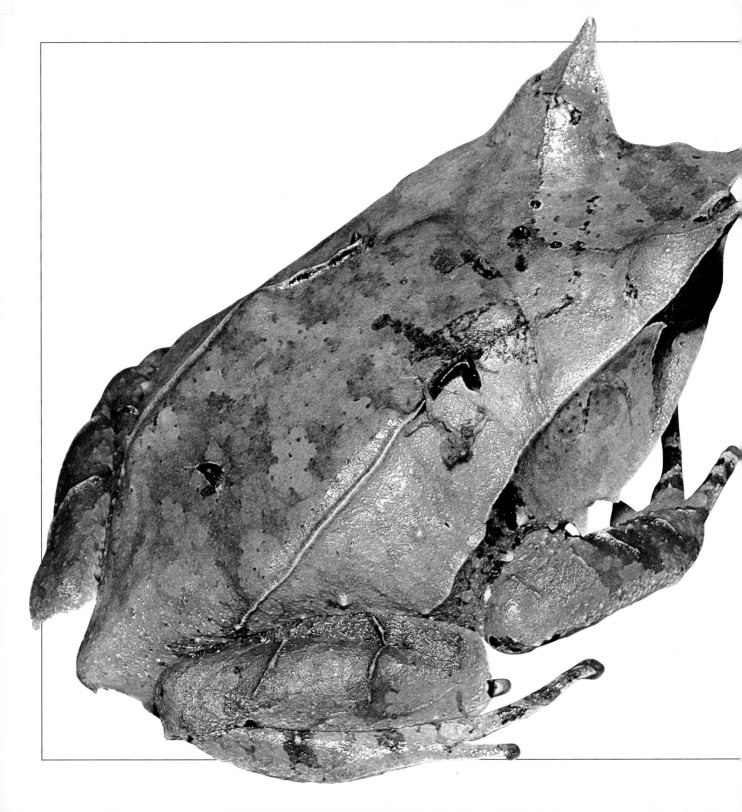

Which animal pretends it is a leaf?

The horned frog lives among the leaves on the forest floor. It is very difficult to see because it looks just like a dead, brown leaf itself. It has brown patches on its body and a line down its back, like the thick vein down the middle of a leaf.

Which bird pretends it's a branch?

The tawny frogmouth rests on a tree branch. The markings on its feathers match the tree bark so closely that the bird looks exactly like a stumpy, broken branch.

Which animals lose their spots as they grow up?

Baby lions have spotted coats which match the broken light shining through the grass and trees. The spots fade as the animals get older and need less protection.

Can a leopard change its spots?

A leopard has its spots for life.
They help to hide it from its prey.
Some leopards, though, are
born black. They are called
black panthers. You can still just
see their spots if the sunlight falls
on their coats.

Which animals pretend to be dead to avoid attack?

Grass snakes don't have a poisonous bite but they have a clever way of defending themselves. If they are in danger, they play dead. They roll over, with their mouths wide open and their tongues hanging out. When the attacker moves off, they quickly come back to life again!

Which snake cheats at camouflage?

The harmless milk snake pretends it is a deadly poisonous coral snake to scare off enemies. It mimics the coral snake's bright red, yellow and black colors. It does not get the pattern quite right but it is good enough to keep attackers away!

Which animal looks like a pebble?

Stonefish live on the floor of the ocean. Their slimy, stone-colored bodies blend in with the pebbles and rocks, making the fish almost impossible to see. If they are stepped on, though, they shoot out deadly poison through sharp spines on their backs.

Which fish looks like seaweed?

The leafy sea dragon has ragged fins and a yellow-green body. It looks exactly like a strand of the seaweed through which it swims.

Which insect has two heads to fool its enemies?

Birds peck butterflies on the head to kill them. So hairstreak butterflies fool birds into attacking their tails. They have long strands, like false antennae, on their back wings. The bird pecks at these instead of the real ones. The butterfly escapes with slightly damaged wings but is still alive.

Which animal pretends to have a frightening face to fool predators?
This frog has two large bumps on its back. They look just like huge, staring eyes. The frog flashes its false eyes at enemies to scare them away.

Why do polar bears cover their black noses?

A scientist studying polar bears in the Arctic discovered that they cover their black noses with their white paws. He decided that the reason for this must be to keep them from showing up against the snow when tracking their prey.

Which animals turn white in winter?

Arctic foxes, weasels and hares change color according to the time of year. They are brown in summer to match the bare, rocky ground. In winter their fur turns white to blend in with the snow.

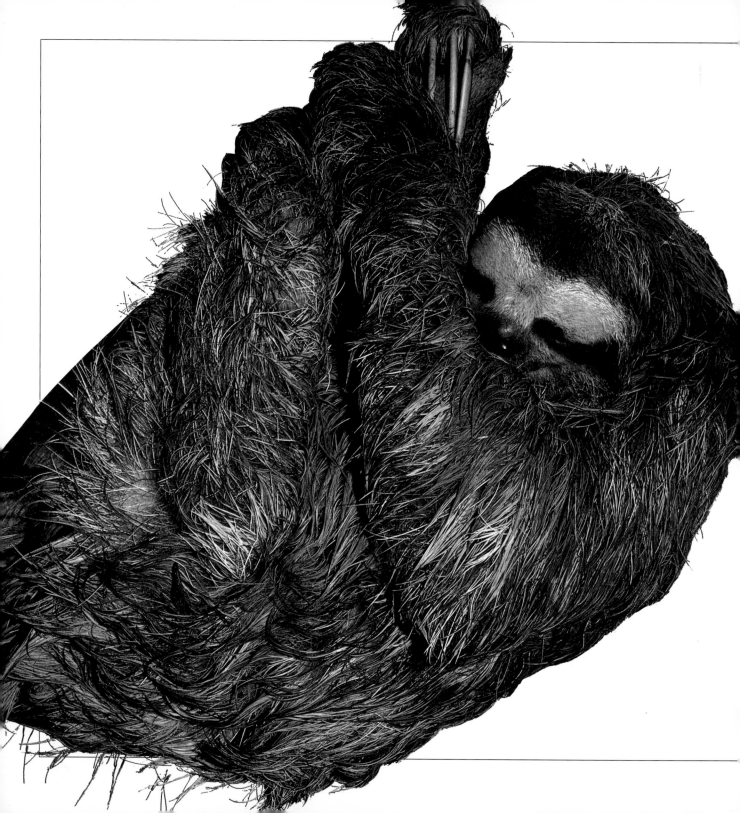

Which animal grows its own camouflage on its hair?

Sloths spend most of their lives hanging upside down in trees. Their hair grows upside down too. You would have to stroke a sloth from its belly to its back. They so rarely wash their hair that tiny green plants, called algae, grow on it. The plants help to camouflage the sloths among the leaves.

Which animal borrows its camouflage?

Spider crabs snip off bits of seaweed and sponges and arrange them on their shells for camouflage. If the crab moves to a leafier part of the sea, it puts extra seaweed on its shell, to hide it better. This is a good example of adapting camouflage to suit changing surroundings.

Index

Photographs
Cover and pages 8/9, 12/13: Bruce Coleman; pages 5, 14, 15, 18, 23: Planet Earth; Pages 7, 21, 24: Frank Lane Picture Agency; pages 10/11: Survival Anglia; pages 16, 26/27, 28: Oxford Scientific Films; page 19: Telegraph Colour Library.